13 Challenges

13 Challenges by Sydney Richardson.
Published by Sydney Richardson
1130 Norwood Ln.
Lewisville, NC 27023

www.raeofknowledge.com

Cover by Herbert Richardson, Jr.

ISBN-13: 978-0-578-49567-5

Keywords: Self-help; Professional Development; Leadership

ABOUT THE BOOK

Children often cannot wait to grow up. The thought is that when a person reaches adulthood, everything will be great because that person can do anything, anytime, anywhere. There are no restraints when someone matures to adulthood. Then – adulthood hits. Add to a person's normal day of getting up, getting dressed, working, and having additional roles and responsibilities such as business-owner, spouse, parent, animal owner, community leader, caretaker of elderly parents, leader in *any* vicinity (even thankless ones), and it's clear to see and understand how a molehill turns into a mountain. All of a sudden that person wishes for the joys of childhood (even a glorified, imaginary one).

Regardless of where you are in life, this book is designed for you, offering tools to help you along your journey of endless responsibilities. The advice and suggestions given in this book may seem incredibly simple. As you read some of the sections, you may have a "duh" moment. But, that's the point. The lessons provided in this book are often the forgotten ones because they are incredibly practical. The problem is that as life becomes more overwhelming, it's easy to forget the tools that keep you grounded and at peace. So, this book serves as your reminder.

Note: 13 Challenges is short on purpose because when you are on a mission, you might not have time to devour a 300-page book. Therefore, use this book when you need it, gleaning lessons in pockets of time.

TABLE OF CONTENTS

MANAGE TIME – IT CAN NOT BE CONTROLLED

"This is the key to time management-to see the value in every moment."
– Menachem Mendel Schneerson

We all know that we are only allotted 168 hours per week to accomplish our "to do" list (if you didn't know, now you do). I love time management workshops because each facilitator reminds me of the actual amount of time I've got, and I get to see what my life looks like on paper. Sometimes, it is a pretty picture, with my hours filled with tasks, followed by a couple of hours of rest. Oftentimes, it is not pretty at all, like the time I scheduled myself for 183 hours! At those less than perfect moments, I realize that there has been poor planning on my part, or I left out a vital step in my week. Once, I planned out the time it would take me to complete an annual report for my job. I had a nicely laid out schedule, but I did not plan on being so mentally exhausted that I needed a nap in the evenings. Can you guess how that threw off the rest of my commitments? Everyone has a moment when they realize that everything can't be done. That is when we learn to manage our time.

My Moment
In the midst of working long hours, while advancing my degree, I had not yet learned how to successfully plan my days and nights. Because of this, my nightly ritual was to crawl into bed in the wee morning hours and get a brief nap before starting the day again. After years of doing this, plus adding more responsibilities to my life, it became normal for me to have muscle spasms, headaches, and knots all over my body. Any of this ring a bell? I had a hard time admitting that I was overworked, sleep deprived, and stressed. So, what did I do? I gave myself a pep talk by saying: "Plenty of people have more hectic lives than I do. Surely I can handle this." **Do not give yourself this talk!** It is unhealthy and unhelpful. It wasn't until a good (and direct) friend of mine helped me face this fact, and I knew that I had to make a change for the better. Thus, the concept of managing what I could made more sense.

The Concept

We're all given the same number of hours in a week—168. That's it. No one gets more. You can't spin around in a circle and get more time. You cannot click your heels together and make more time appear. So, you've got to decide what to do with the time you have, and adjust. Here are a few things you can do to better manage the time chaos:

- First things first- you may have learned this early in life, and it remains to be true: <u>finish large projects first.</u> Get it out of the way so the hardest part is over. There's no point in staring at something major all day long. Get it done; if you have to, get it done in parts- a little bit every day. The more you chomp away, the faster it diminishes. Save the routine tasks for later because you can probably do them with your eyes closed.
- Say "no"- this is a tough one for so many reasons. It's just easier to say "yes" and gripe about the task later. But, if you truly want to take better care of yourself and accomplish your work and dreams, you've GOT to say no sometimes. No more, "I'll try to make it" or "Let me get back to you", or "Sure!" while loathing yourself later. Just politely say "no" and that's it! Don't offer an explanation either. Your answer is "no" and no one needs to know why.

Disclaimer: Mentally and emotionally prepare yourself for pushback from others. This is a normal response from people.

- Delegate- do you *have* to do everything yourself? Will the world fall to pieces if someone else takes over? If the answer is "yes" (which is usually not true) then you'll never gain the time you truly need. Look at your list of to-dos. Which items can be put off for later or completed by someone else? Who can you ask for assistance? If you have no one to delegate to (I understand that this happens sometimes), break your tasks into parts on a calendar, so you'll have a realistic picture of how long each commitment will take to complete. From there, tackle one project at a time.

- Schedule time for yourself- this seems simple, yet it doesn't get done. Look at your weekly calendar right now. Go ahead, I'll

6

wait (if you don't have a calendar, you'll start one by the end of this book). Now, schedule a moment for yourself this week. It can be for 15 minutes, 30 minutes, or an hour—your choice. Got it? Guess what? You don't have to worry about making time for yourself this week! You've already set an appointment that you **will** keep.

*The rest of this book expands on these concepts and others.

Challenge: Calculate how many hours you actually use during the week. If it's over 168, start by reducing or eliminating some hours. If it's exactly 168, still reduce some hours. If it's fewer than 168, but it doesn't incorporate time for yourself or an outlet/hobby that you enjoy, schedule that time.

Here are some categories to consider for your calendar: sleep, eating/food prep, travel, work, exercise, getting ready in the morning. These items take up more time than you think. Good luck!

MAKE TIME FOR YOURSELF!

"Almost everything will work again if you unplug it for a few minutes...including you."
- Anne Lamott

The previous segment had you schedule time within 168 hours, so let's delve deeper into this. In the midst of everything already happening in your life, when was the last time you scheduled regular, consistent time for yourself? If you haven't, then forget about putting first things first, delegating tasks, or saying no to others. Why? Because you will become overtired, overworked, and extremely frustrated since you've spent time taking care of everyone and everything else, except yourself.

I'd like to tell you about T. T is a single parent who works a full-time job, as well as a part-time job. Actually, for as long as I've known her, she's always worked and taken care of others. During her teenage years, she worked in her parent's business and watched over her younger siblings. She worked throughout high school and while getting her advanced degree. As a single parent, she continues to work hard, but she is also the "go-to" person whenever her extended family needs anything (a place to stay, a babysitter, a caregiver to another family member, etc.). T is constantly willing to and ready to lend a hand or an extra room, all while taking care of herself and her child. Yet, while she cares for everyone else, who takes care of her? You guessed it.

If you were to ask T when she actually gets time to herself, her answer would be, "whenever I can." What's wrong with that response? Well, if you've ever tried to live by that principle, you would know that "whenever I can" turns into "never" because someone always needs you. Taking time to yourself requires you *making* it happen.

Many people assume that taking care of themselves involves scheduling hours in an already hectic week. It does not. Start with scheduling 15 minutes for yourself in one week. For some, this may seem like a small amount of time, but it is imperative to start small.

I began scheduling 15 minutes to myself on Friday nights. For those minutes, I didn't talk on the phone, clean the house, finish work, play with the kids, or get a head start on Saturday errands. It was *my* time to relax and it helped! I became excited knowing that when I looked at my weekly calendar, I had a scheduled time just for me! Pretty soon, this increased to 30 minutes a week. Then 30 minutes every few days. Now, I take time to myself daily. I'll admit, sometimes life gets in the way, but because I've made an appointment with myself, it's easier to get back on track. The same can happen for you! Taking time does not have to be luxurious either. It can be walking outside, exercising, listening to music, or locking yourself in your room and enjoying a favorite treat (chocolate and wine anyone?). So, let's get started.

Choosing the day
Think about your week. What is your lightest day of the week? This is a great place to start taking time for yourself. For example, if you normally work a 12-hour day, choose a day where you're only working 10 hours. Once again, start with 15 minutes and book that appointment with yourself!

Choosing the time
Now pick a time you can commit to. Are you an early riser? If so, your mornings are where your 15 minutes should go. Consider coffee on the porch before the rest of the house wakes. Are you a night owl? Before working at night, take 15 minutes to unplug and do something just for yourself. If you're a midday person, consider taking a walk during your lunch hour, or during a time where you're often not as needed by others. Do not say that you're always needed. Chances are, you're not (people are just demanding). Either delegate items to someone else for 15 minutes or (GASP) let people wait.

Choosing the space
Now comes the trickier part: the space. This is especially for those of you who will be at home, surrounded by others, during your 15 or 30 minutes of alone time. Where can you go where you won't be bothered? Naturally, you'll always be bothered at some point, but don't stop thinking about it. Look around your home. Where can you

be alone for a while? The next point is significant for making this happen.

Letting people around you know
For those with families at home: communicating your needs with your family is important. There's no point in telling your family that you're taking time for yourself if you don't exercise that opportunity. Therefore, once you've chosen your designated area (assuming the rest of the house is awake) let your family know what you need from them: to be left alone for X amount of time. But then you have to do it! Others **will forget** that you're beginning this, so it's important to establish this practice and keep it up.

The same goes for those who live alone, but have family, friends, significant others, and colleagues always calling. Think about telling them that between certain times in the day, you will not be taking available. Oh the shame!

Two-part challenge: Part I- Choose a time, place, and day to begin scheduling time for yourself.

Part II- Let others know your plans.

Part III- Turn your devices off! I did not mention this earlier, but part of taking time for yourself involves not answering calls, checking email, or doing anything that will distract you. Say goodbye to distractions (good or bad) for at least 15 minutes. Good luck!

SOMETIMES YOU NEED A DAY

Making yourself a priority is necessary in life.

I once had a breakfast meeting with a friend who was clearly overwhelmed with her schedule. As a person who worked full-time, was the first point of contact for her aging parents, and who was starting her own business, she had a set of justifiable commitments *and* complaints. This person was completely capable of anything and everything she put her mind to, but I was not expecting the water works that eventually accompanied her complaints. She was extremely tired and felt as though she wasn't good enough because she couldn't handle everything on her plate. I sympathized with her and, at the same time, related to her need to take on the world with a broken smile. So, I suggested that we look at her typical week.

As we reviewed her days, I began to see a light at the end of the tunnel, but she did not. So, I suggested something radical (using the term loosely), and I'm suggesting it to you as well. When I made my suggestion, she looked at me with horror because it simply did not fit with her workaholic nature. But, what happens when you need a serious break? What do you do when your body looks halfway contorted because you're incredibly stressed out? My suggestion was to **drop everything and take a day or two for herself.**

You may be thinking, "AHHHHH!!!!!! But I'll miss work and that's bad!" Maybe, but I'm sure your boss would rather have you miss work than receive a call from the hospital because you had heart attack. Also, if you're that overworked or stressed out, then it's safe to say that you have some vacation and sick days stored up. To put it simply, when you are too stressed to function as you normally would, it's time to take a break. Believe it or not, we can also pre-plan for this. I taught my friend how to do this because I learned to do this years ago. Ready?

- Plan out your entire year first. What major events are coming up? What work/volunteer/ community projects have you agreed to complete? Every year, I have a good idea of which month will be "hell month" and which week(s) will be "hell

11

week(s)" for me. These are the months and weeks of nonstop events that simply have to get done. There's no way out of it, so I schedule those first. Then I plan around them.

- The week before and the week after your major event(s) should be easier weeks. Pre-plan to do the bare minimum during those times, which may mean only following a basic, daily schedule- but no extras! No dinners out, no last-minute birthday parties. Nothing.

- Schedule the equivalent of one weekend (or at least 1 day) every month for rest and relaxation. **Note: rest and relaxation looks different to each person.** This is bigger than the standard 15-30 minutes. This is time for your body to recharge. Take a nap, get a massage, go for a hike, lay around the house and watch television. Do something that does not involve working or serving others.

By following these three steps, you avoid running the risk of needing to leave work early or getting sick repeatedly because your body is giving you warning signs. Our bodies can respond to stress before we realize what is stressing us out, so do yourself a favor and implement preventative strategies.

Challenge: Take the 3 steps mentioned above and get a head start on planning your next six months, at least. Do you have any crazy weeks or months coming up? Recognize those and plan around them. Good luck!

THE 5 PEOPLE YOU NEED IN LIFE

Everyone needs a crew.

It was my first class in graduate school, and I was sitting among my peers, ready to learn. Our professor entered the classroom and gave us all an assignment. She said, "Tell me who's a part of your support system." While some classmates listed a number of people, I had a hard time coming up with my list. I knew that I had family and friends who supported me in life, but it was hard for me to explain the specific roles that each person played, or how they exactly supported me outside of listening to me vent or offering advice from time to time. My professor never told us how many people needed to be in our support system, but he really made our class reflect on the relationships in our lives and what they meant to *and* for us.

In order to succeed in life, we all need a support team. Now, when giving talks either to a group or to individuals, I always ask people to tell me about the people on their support team. I have discovered that I hear one of two main things when I receive an answer from people: 1) everyone has people on their team, but they don't always know that person's purpose (and it's usually family and friends on their team), or 2) there's no one on a person's team. Therefore, most people are going through life with people surrounding them, but they may not know each person's role in their life.

While having family and friends on your support team is good, you need to know the role that they play in your life, and there should be people outside of family and friends who are a part of this support system. This could be colleagues, people in the community, and/or others from various social circles. Over the years, this list will grow, but start with a least five people whom you can confide in and receive direction from. These five people, otherwise known as *The Incredible 5,* should have specific roles on your team. They do not have to be friends with one another because that is not the point. The point is for you to have a select group of people who contribute to your life's direction and purpose. So, let's look at who these people are:

The Incredible 5
There are 5 people you need on your list.

- The Cheerleader- this is the person who's always in your corner, regardless of the circumstance. This person believes fully in your capability and is ready and willing to throw those pom-poms in the air every time you embark on a new adventure in life.

- The Coach- this is your guide. Some people call this person your mentor. Your coach is someone who helps guide your path and keeps you focused on the big picture and end goal(s).

- The Devil's Advocate- this is not a negative person, but someone who doesn't mind challenging you. Are you sure you want to fly to Hawaii for a five-day vacation when you just started your job? Why don't you wait until your scheduled vacation starts? This person loves you deeply, but isn't afraid of you getting mad when they play devil's advocate.

- The Listener- everyone needs a listener. This is someone who may not comment at all, but just let you talk. You can vent, dream, and even answer your own questions. It doesn't matter because this person is happy to let you voice your worries and/or opinions, and this person realizes that talking things out is powerful.

- The One with Childlike gusto (AKA 'the child') – This one is my favorite because this person keeps you excited about life. 'The child' is the one who is successful, but may not have gone the traditional route. This person encourages you to take risks, and play hard. This person never lets you forget that your life is interesting and you have something to be excited about.

In my case, everyone on my team doesn't know they're a part of it, and they don't have to. That's not the point. The point is to have reliable people who you can go to when you need them.

So, who's on your support team? If you don't have one, then you already know what your task is: create a support team. List them by name and role. Good luck!

SAY "NO"

"Saying no can be the ultimate self-care."
– Claudia Black

I wish I could say that I learned this lesson early in my career, but I can't. I learned this lesson when I realized that it was my responsibility to set my own boundaries. If I continued not to, I couldn't get angry at others for constantly taking advantage of me.

Saying "no" is hard for some people and it's understandable as to why. We don't want to offend anyone. We don't want to hurt one another's feelings. If our reason for saying "no" is simply because we don't want to do what we are being asked, then we feel guilty for being selfish, and say "yes" in spite of our feelings.

But guess what? Saying "no" is perfectly alright. It doesn't mean you're being rude. It doesn't mean that you don't care. It simply means that something was offered to you in which you do not want to participate. What's wrong with that? Absolutely nothing.

Now, as a disclaimer: There are times when saying yes, even though we do not want to do something, is important. I may not want to be surrounded by 20 five-year olds, but I'm still going to host my child's birthday party. I may not feel like writing a report for my boss, but I'm not going to say "no" to it because that's part of my job.

So aside from special cases, let's look at three ways to say no.

- Get comfortable saying, "Let me consider this," but don't take too long. This is good if you *truly* want to think about the proposition. If, in your gut, you do not want to participate, then go back to the person and say, "Thank you for the offer, but I'm not interested." Here's the key- you will be asked to explain yourself or you will be offered another scenario. Confidently say no without explanation, which brings me to the next item.

- Say no without an explanation: We get caught and get sucked into saying "yes" because the person that asked has now

16

requested/demanded an explanation for our denial. It's a trick by the person asking us for a favor and that person knows it! So, your job is to say "no thank you." When asked why, simply say one of two things (depending on your level of comfort): 1) I'm not interested or 2) I have something else to do. You will be asked what else you have to do and at this point, you can politely say, "that's personal." Why? Because the person asking does not care what you have to do; that person's just trying to find a way to rope you in to agreeing to the original ask. Don't let them. Do not give an explanation.

- Practice, practice, practice. Let's face it, practice makes perfect. Walk around your house practicing saying "no." Try it out with a friend (seriously). The more you practice, the more confident you'll become in saying this word without feeling guilty.

So, here's your challenge: Practice saying no, but here's the catch: Don't just walk around saying "no." Practice saying it to people who you feel you can't say no to. Believe me, an opportunity will arise. Good Luck!

DELEGATE

"Delegating work works, provided the one delegating works, too."
– Robert Half

There are three phenomenal people in my life who have pushed me to better myself in so many ways (professionally, emotionally, spiritually, physically). Here's the thing: they all share the same flaw. They are HORRIBLE at delegating! These three people are perfectionists and workaholics. They believe that the world will crumble and they will be judged by a high court if they don't 1) do everything themselves, or 2) stand over the person they've delegated tasks to, watching them to ensure perfection. Okay, so I may have exaggerated the last one, but not by much. These people have a hard time fully delegating tasks because they need to be in control, and that need has caused them much stress, sleepless nights, and overworked days.

In our time pressed, get-it-done culture, people have been conditioned to believe that work must be completed "right here and right now." Work-related stress is all too common, along with its physical and mental affects. Add home life and/or community obligations to the mix, and you have a surefire recipe for disaster for those who have not learned to delegate tasks.

Some people are great at delegating, but those of us who favor control have a hard time letting other people take on even small tasks. If you're going to be a leader on your job, in your home, your community, or in any organization, you've got to learn to delegate.

Let me rephrase: if you're going to live life with a little less stress, you'll need to learn to delegate. Delegating does not mean *not* doing any work. It means giving smaller tasks to people so you can focus on other parts of your work (i.e. larger projects). But, the major part is deciding what to delegate and to whom?

What to delegate?
Ask yourself this: Do you have to do everything yourself? Will your boss fire you or will your significant other dismiss you if you don't do everything **yourself**? If your answer is 'no' (which it should be) then

there are areas that can be handed off to others. Decide what these are and who around you can help. The goal is to get things done.

To start, delegate small areas of your tasks to others. For example, if you have two major projects that need to be completed for work, but small parts incorporate making copies or researching minor areas, delegate those tasks to a staff member (if they're available). This allows you to focus on major sections of your work. Now, think of various areas of your life for the next section.

How to delegate?
- This is the hard part. The first thing to do is to think of people who are reliable enough to complete minor tasks. I'm not asking you to consider people who will do things *your* way, only people who will complete the assignment given. This list may have one or two people on it, but as long as you have someone listed, then you've got something to work with.

- Now, you've got to ask. Let whoever you choose know that you'd like assistance and tell them what you'd like them to do. At work, it should be an assistant or someone in your department. Be ready to give assistance when they need you as well. Now, you've not only set up people who can help you, but you've also established relationship with others.

- Provide instructions. There's nothing worse than being given an assignment with less than clear instructions. In order to "loosen the reigns" a bit, and feel at ease about it, it's important to leave instructions to the person completing your work. Be as clear and detailed as possible.

- Once the task is completed, place it to the side and **schedule** a day and time to review the work. Once the work is reviewed, meet with the person who completed it and discuss their performance and the outcome of the assignment. Not only have you delegated responsibility, but you've helped to develop another person's skills.

Things that cannot be delegated

Unfortunately, there are some items that cannot be given to other people and truly have to be done by you. There is also the reality that not everyone has people to delegate tasks to, at work or at home. Let's be honest, sometimes delegating means paying a person, and not everyone has additional monies for this (ex. housekeeper or virtual assistant). If this is the case, then it's important to prioritize. Do all of the items have to be done in one day, or can they be spread across a couple of days? More than likely, they can be spread across multiple days or even weeks, which is great! This means that you will be less overwhelmed. In that case, attack the major item(s) first and work down to the smallest item, but be creative. For example,

- For the home, order groceries online and pick them up after work or on the weekend.

- Have groceries delivered to your home.

- Exchange services with a friend (ex. You dog-sit in exchange for a friend's typing services).

- You perform a task for a colleague now in exchange for that person completing a task for you later on (know of any upcoming projects?).

Regardless of the duty to be performed, you should always find ways to delegate, especially if you have more work than hours available.

Time for a challenge: Choose, at minimum, two tasks for the week or month to delegate to someone else. Remember, this is not about having things done your way, but getting more tasks completed. Good luck!

ASK FOR HELP

"The only mistake you can make is not asking for help."
– Sandeep Jauhar

I remember sitting in my graduate class, waiting one Saturday morning for everyone to arrive. It was going to be a loooong day. At the time I registered for the course, I thought I'd have more free time on my hands, but that wasn't the case. So, there I was, sitting at my desk and kicking myself because I forgot to pack a lunch. I was dressed in sweats, my hair was in a bun, and I literally looked like I had rolled out of bed. Who would care anyway, I thought. We're all students here and I have to dress up when I go to work, so I can take a sloppy day.

At that moment, more students walked into the classroom, and I noticed two women who chose to sit on either side of me. The woman on my left was dressed in a red and white patterned, flowing dress. Her hair was shiny without a strand out of place, her backpack was filled neatly and orderly, and she had her lunch bag with her. The woman on the right side of me was equally beautifully dressed, with her manicured nails, briefcase, and mini cooler for her lunch. There were more nicely kept people in the class, but I noticed these two women in particular since they were so close to me. Surely they were coming from a convention, I thought.

During our lunch break (when I bought a bag of chips), the three of us had a conversation about what we did. I found out that both women were principals: one was a single mother and the other was married with a teenager and a toddler. Her spouse was in administration and in graduate school as well. I was astonished! How was it that I looked and felt as though I had been hit with a truck, yet these women were fully put together with just as many or more responsibilities than me?

I wanted to ask them how they did it, but I couldn't (not at that time, anyway). Feeling ashamed, I could not admit that I needed help, let alone ask for help or guidance—from anyone. Sound familiar? The truth is that there are multiple reasons why people don't ask for assistance, but here are a few common ones:

- We're afraid of seeming incompetent. We simply don't want anyone else to know that we don't have it all together.

- We don't know <u>who</u> to ask. We may know what we need, but who should we go to?

- We don't know <u>what</u> to ask. This is huge because we often don't know what questions need to be asked in order to receive the best help.

I fell into each category until I reached a point where something had to give or else I was going to explode. So, one day during our lunch period, I asked each woman how she managed to have everything in order. Their stories and advice were invaluable and helped me tremendously. There are still times when I have trouble asking for help, but there are some things I've done to make it easier for me and I've advised others to do the same.

- Consider reading about the topic you'd like assistance with. We're incredibly lucky to not only have books, but the internet which touches on any topic we can imagine. Need help organizing your house? There are articles and videos on it. Need help with study habits? Books and videos galore. Want information about negotiating a salary? Pick a place to begin. Reading about a topic and what others have done can give us some much-needed guidance in areas where we lack knowledge.

- Make friends or become acquaintances with people you admire. You'll not only build relationships, but you may have something to offer them as well. We can always learn from one another.

- Once you feel more confident in yourself, you'll be able to seek direct assistance. But, seek assistance from people you trust and from people who are succeeding in areas you strive to succeed in as well.

Challenge: What is something you've had trouble asking for help with? What are some steps you can take this week to get the

advice and assistance you need? Make a list, along with some steps and get started. Good luck!

HAVE A BACKUP PLAN

You don't make a plan to guarantee things go smoothly; you create a plan to make life smoother.

It was my first year at a new job. I was in a new environment, surrounded by new people, a new schedule, new germs, and no "what if" plan. I got up every morning, went to work, went home, and started my day again. I didn't bother to keep up with a calendar of my daily activities because it was all in my head; therefore, I had no backup plan in case anything went wrong.

Well, things went wrong. A lot of things! I got sick six different times throughout the year because my immune system wasn't as strong as I thought. A family death occurred during one of the busiest weeks in the year, and I had no one to cover for me at work (plus, I was an emotional wreck). And finally, during the winter, my car suddenly decided that it wasn't going to start until the sun shined on it for at least two hours! True story.

I quickly learned that it wasn't only important to have a plan, but to have a backup plan (and a backup plan for the backup plan). The problem was that, at that time in my life, I considered myself to be a free spirit. Free spirits didn't have plans, or so I thought. It wasn't until I learned that not having a plan stopped me from being as *free spirited* as I wanted to be, so I finally gave in—and I haven't been happier.

As life gets busier, it becomes unrealistic to expect that you can take care of yourself, others, accomplish your day-to-day responsibilities, and achieve your dreams without planning at least a portion of it on paper. That was fine as an adolescent, but it is dangerous as an adult. Having a roadmap, and a backup roadmap does not mean that your plans won't change. It does, however, mean that when those plans change, they can still align with the rest of your vision.

Myths vs. Truths

There are many myths surrounding having a plan, so let's separate the myths from the truths.

- *Plans mean everything will go perfectly!* Actually, emergencies will still happen and distractions will arise. Plans just give us a roadmap to come back to when we veer off track.

- *Plans make my life so predictable and that's no fun.* Well, in some ways, your life *is* predictable on a day-to-day basis. Having a set plan allows room for fun without worrying if you missed anything at home, work, with family, etc.

- *Plans mean that I have to follow a step by step routine.* Honestly, you do not have to follow your plan step by step. It acts in two ways: 1) as a list of goals for your day, month, and year, and 2) as a guideline of steps to follow when things don't go accordingly. It's better to have an idea of where you're going than to travel blindly.

Questions to answer

To know whether or not you need a backup plan, consider the following questions:

1. If your car died over night, how would you get to work or get your errands accomplished?

2. **For parents:** If your child runs into your room at 4 am with a high fever, would you be in a panic about things that needed to get done, or would you have a plan of attack?

3. Who's on your list of "backup people" to help you if anything goes wrong in your life? Do you even have a list of backup people?

4. Is there anyone on your job who knows what to do if you can't make it into work? Do you have a list of daily activities or instructions for them, just in case?

25

If you can't answer "yes" to any of these questions confidently, or if you can't answer questions 1 and 3, then you've got something to work on. Your answers are essential to having your tail covered as much as possible. Remember, this is about making sure things go smoother than they would without a roadmap. **Challenge: Use the questions to start your What If plan. Good luck**

IDENTIFY YOUR OUTLET

"People with many interests live, not only the longest, but the happiest."
-    George Matthew Allen

So far, we've covered managing time, delegating tasks, and scheduling 15 minutes to yourself, so let's tackle something that plagues many busy people: not having an outlet or hobbies. While we laugh about it now, my sister and I used to have Friday evening conversations, covering the week's events. I ran down my list of things I did and she ran down her list. One evening, I told her that I noticed that her list of weekend activities seemed, more or less, work related. "What do you do for fun?" I asked her. She then told me what was fun for her. I reiterated that everything she listed was actually more work, especially since others expected her to complete the tasks she mentioned. Fast forward 15 minutes later in the conversation, and we established that she was in fact constantly working, even when she sometimes enjoyed it.

As we move through life, it becomes very easy for our days and weekends to somehow revolve around work, family, and community, almost until we don't realize what parts of our lives are just about us. When life becomes too busy, what's the first thing to go? Those things that were enjoyment for us only (leisurely reading, the gym, art, social clubs, sports, etc.) are first to get marked out. They are the first thing to go because we convince ourselves that we'll get back to them eventually, when we have time.

The truth is that our lives become busier, and we never actually have time to enjoy those things that we put to the side *for a moment*. But, everyone needs an outlet, something that is just for them that they enjoy. It's not work-related, and it doesn't involve being of service to another person, even if you enjoy doing it. If thinking of doing something just for yourself that is fun sounds selfish to you, then I am asking you (actually challenging you) to be selfish. Therefore, my question is simple, but the answer may be difficult: what is your outlet? What do you do for fun that has absolutely nothing to do with work, family, responsibility, or accountability? If you have an outlet, how often do you indulge in it?

Years after the above conversation with my sister, I could no longer answer those questions when she asked me about my outlet. Somehow over time, my work and home life became my only life, and I couldn't pinpoint when this had taken place. It took a while for me to figure out what I enjoyed again, and then it took longer to make it a regular practice.

Outlet Exercise
If you're having a difficult time knowing what your outlet would be, first know that this is not uncommon. It's normal for life and work to merge to a point where 1) you can't tell one apart from the other, and 2) what you thought were your outlets (ex. Fundraising events) were actually other parts of your job. Consider the questions below when figuring out your hobby and interests:

- You're on vacation for a week with no computer or phone. What are you doing for fun?

- What did you enjoy doing as a child?

- What are you interested in that you'd like to pursue if money was no object?

- The rules of income have suddenly changed where you could only earn money by focusing on your hobbies. What are your hobbies?

Challenge: Answer these questions, and once you establish your outlets, find time in your schedule (you should have a draft of one by now) to take part in them. You'll be glad you did. Good luck!

SAY "YES"

"I learned to always take on things I'd never done before. Growth and comfort do not coexist."
- Ginni Rometty

Don't throw the book! I know that I told you to say "no" a few sections ago, and now I'm telling you to say "yes." I promise you, it's not the same thing. You're not saying yes to everything; you're saying yes to opportunity. Whenever I would hear someone speak about success, or read about success, the same idea tended to arise: learn to say "no." The speaker or author would then explain why saying "no" was essential to one's life, and it would usually involve the following reasons: 1) saying "no" protected one's time; 2) saying "no" was empowering and allowed the person to retain control. Now, all of these reasons are important, especially if one does not have enough time to commit to another task. I even advised people about the power of "no", and I believe in it, but I also believe in the power of "yes."

I reflected on my own life paths (i.e. education, family, career, personal and professional relationships, etc.). Then, I began talking to other people about their life journeys to success and I realized that we shared a similarity that people rarely talked about. We often said "yes" to requests that came our way.

Confession Time

Allow me to paint a picture of this for you. I have yet to have a job or position on a board, council, or committee that someone did not invite me to apply for or join. Here is my admission – I am extremely indecisive about anything that pertains to my life. I have a hard time deciding a path for myself (although I can easily do it for others). I question and double question every decision I make for fear that I will make the wrong choice. But, over the years, I noticed that other people saw strengths and talents in me that I never paid attention to, or never knew I had. When I reflected on my life path, I noticed that I rarely moved without the coaxing of someone else, and I had enough sense to say "yes" to those opportunities and tasks that others offered me. Those tasks, even tedious ones that no one else wanted, led me to greater opportunities, both personally and professionally.

Open Doors

When I spoke with other people whom I considered to be models of success, I would hear the same thing. One executive claimed that he took a job he was not fully interested in because it was an opportunity to expand his skills. Someone suggested it to him because that person felt that he was perfect for the job. As a result, he is in a position that he now enjoys and has been sought out for various other positions.

A former colleague said "yes" to a one-year position that she would not have normally taken. That one-year position led to other opportunities that she felt may not have come her way had she said "no." Saying "yes" can lead to development of skills, attainment of new ones, meeting incredible people, and walking through doors that might not open in other settings.

So why is the focus constantly on saying "no"? Saying "no" allows a level of protection and an element of control over one's time. It prevents us from being people pleasers and affords us the chance to consciously decide how we want to spend our time (instead of those around us deciding it for us). Learning to say "no" is actually good for people who are apprehensive about hurting the feelings of others or letting others down.

But, for those who have already set their limits and are ready to experience growth, I challenge you to say "yes" to opportunities that come your way.

This does not mean that you agree to everything offered, but it does mean that you allow room for unexpected chances to arise. Be willing to take notes for a committee. Apply for that volunteer position that has been open for the past year, and be loyal to it. You never know who you may meet or what you may learn that could lead to your next adventure.

Challenge: Over the next month, say "yes" to one opportunity that comes your way, and fully embrace it.

DON'T LET FEAR RULE YOU

"What you are afraid to do is a clear indication of the next thing you need to do."
– Ralph Waldo Emerson

A wonderful friend of mine (let's call her Brenda) was offered a job she greatly wanted. When she called to tell me about it, she sounded excited, but I also sensed nervousness in her voice. Because she had been at her current job for a few years, and had grown attached to her staff and clients, she was apprehensive about leaving for another job, even though it was a better opportunity. As we talked through her nervousness, it became very clear what she should do: take the new job.

After letting her know that her feelings about leaving the safety of her current job was normal, I also let her know the main theme I had picked out from her voicing her thoughts: her reason for possibly not taking the new job was fear of the unknown.

Can you guess what my advice was? "Don't let fear rule you. Don't let fear be the reason that you don't move onto the next adventure."

Fear is a natural emotion and we should pay attention to it and assess from where it stems. Once that has been figured out, it's important to make the next decision based on where fear stems, not from fear itself. Fear has the power to stop a person from progressing in life. That halt can lead to resentment and anger. While fear is healthy, it's important that one doesn't allow fear to become a debilitating factor in one's life.

So, what should we do when facing fear?
- Acknowledge that fear is present. Take as long as you need, but recognize that it has shown up.

- Feel it. Too often, I have witnessed people do one of two things: 1) brush fear off because they see it as a weakness, or 2) get so wrapped up in fear that it stops them from making progress in their lives. So, how about meeting fear in the middle? Feel the fear and get comfortable with it. Don't let fear make *you* afraid.

- Decide what the fear means. This is crucial before you move to the next step. Is the fear a sign that you should slow down, or is it a distraction from success? Your answer decides your next step.

- Make a move – if fear is a sign that you need to slow down and reassess some choices, then do just that, and recognize that fear presented itself to help you. If fear is a natural response because you are about to do something new and/or exciting, then recognize it as that (i.e. a distraction) and move forward.

*I also recommend seeking counsel when the decisions aren't easy to make. An objective person can help you figure out your next step.

Challenge: Be prepared for fear to arise. What is something that you are fearful of doing? Follow these four steps above to determine your next course of action.

ESTABLISH ROUTINES

"The secret of your success is found in your daily routine."
-     John Maxwell

Disclaimer: For me, "successful" means that you enjoy the life you have created, and you are productive.

I will never forget the day that my coffeemaker broke as I was preparing for work. My spouse was ready to walk out of the house and the kids were dressed for school. I just needed to grab my cup of coffee, as part of my daily routine, and the day would be set. As I walked into the kitchen, I saw that only a quarter of a cup had brewed. I turned off the machine and restarted it. Nothing happened. I turned off the machine again and unplugged it. I then turned it on and waited. Nothing happened. To some people, this would not have been a big deal. They would have headed to the local coffee shop, grabbed their favorite drink, and all would be right with the world. For me, as someone who makes coffee daily, and needs it as much as I need my air, this was disastrous. It was so bad, that my colleagues recognized that something was wrong when I could barely string a sentence together at work. Needless to say, coffee was a part of my daily routine, and my routine was broken that day (Tea is a close second, but that wasn't in the house.)

There are people who think that having a routine creates a rut that one cannot get out of. While this can be true to an extent, I'm going to argue in favor of creating a routine. When I observe people who are successful, I notice that there are certain things that they do every day or every week. They are consistent with their routines and rarely stray from them. While the rest of their day can be chaotic and surprising (not always in a good way), their routines give them a sense of stability and productivity.

Cameron works 50 hours per week, is a caretaker to her elderly parents, volunteers in her community, and basically operates as the "center" of her own family. You might know the type. She's the person everyone (family, friends, coworkers, etc.) runs to, even if

33

there are other people and resources available to assist them. While Cameron can at times get overwhelmed by this sense of responsibility (and obligation, if we're being honest), she admits that she also enjoys being needed and would not change anything about her life.

After observing her for years, I asked her how she managed to keep going, day after day, as though she's the Energizer Bunny. Her response: Routines. Essentially, there were certain things she did every day and every week that kept her at peace. They set the tone for different parts of her day and served as priorities for her. Some of these things included:

- Running every morning (sometimes as early as 5am);

- Packing her lunch every night;

- Physically checking on her parents once per week (the day may change);

- Paying bills and reviewing mail on Thursday every week;

- Waking up at the same time every day.

As you can see, these aren't major things, but they were priorities for her. Because she automatically scheduled these items every week, she didn't care as much about what happened with her day-to-day life. Your list of consistencies may look different, but it's important to have some routine to your life in order to thrive.

Challenge: Make a list of 3-4 things you HAVE to have in order to function on a daily and weekly basis. Once you have that list, schedule it into your daily and weekly routine.

BE A LIFE-LONG LEARNER

"Life is a learning process, learning is a life-long process; you can't separate them."
- Vivienne Forrester

In my early years as an adult educator, I came to believe that being a life-long learner meant that one had to take courses at a college. Whether it was a credit-bearing course or a non-credit bearing course, I was convinced that learning (at least advanced learning) had to involve a classroom, until I met some remarkable people who showed me that life-long learning take many forms.

I've had the pleasure of meeting company presidents, vice presidents, CEOs, directors, financial advisors, community advisors, and more. They juggle work, life, relationships of all sorts, and community service and engagement. They are all intelligent people who enjoy life and seek out adventure. More importantly, they are not immune to obstacles or challenges, but what makes them so remarkable is that they are life-long learners. There are some things that they all do differently based on preferences, learning styles, abilities, and schedules, but there are a good number of things that they do similarly, which contribute to their learning.

- They are avid readers. These people realize that if they want to gain knowledge, they have to read. Books, articles, blogs, newspapers: you name it, they read it. Reading is a cost-effective way to learn more about a specialized area and to open one's mind to another way of thinking.

- They get involved in their community. Some of them volunteer regularly; others run 5Ks supporting a cause; some serve on boards or councils. Regardless of the avenue, they all make time to learn about their community and become an active member of it, thus learning from it while giving to it.

- They take classes. Not all of these are offered at a college, and not all come with a price. Some classes are for fun while others concern serious topics, but these leaders take classes to learn new skills and gain knowledge, while being around other people with similar interests.

- They all have a favorite radio station or podcast that they listen to. For most of them, it's NPR, but I noticed that they all tune into a show or station for in-depth topic discussion, and to get a more global view of an issue. They aren't just concerned with local thoughts, but also with international thinking because they recognize that there is a global mindset to learn.

As a result, there are certain characteristics that I see in these people that have contributed to their lives. They have an open mindset; engage in civil discourse; they are patient decision-makers; they are confident in voicing their thoughts and defending them; and they are humble. These characteristics have served them well in their lives, and have contributed to their success.

How do you engage in life-long learning? Here are some areas to consider if you want to be a life-long learner:

- Read – in what ways can you expand your reading and when? What are some topics that you know little about, but can expand on?
- Community Engagement- do you stay current on what is taking place in your city? If not, how can you best do this? Are there causes that you can involve yourself in through volunteering or other modes of service?

- Class learning – are there free classes offered in your area that interest you? Are there online classes offered or groups you can join that are of interest to you?

- Global mindset – it would be great to travel, but if you cannot, what resources can you utilize to learn more about the world? Are there any events taking place near you that focus on international issues?

Challenge: After answering these questions, pick one area to focus on in order to be a life-long learner. Choose a way to learn about it. Be sure to record your experience, what was learned, and any new acquaintances you met or opportunities that opened up as a result. Good luck and enjoy!

Notes- jot down ideas or reflections along the way

ABOUT THE AUTHOR

Sydney D. Richardson, Ph.D. has worked in higher education and volunteered for nonprofits for over fifteen years. Her roles have included: instructor, Assistant Professor, Writing Center Director, and Dean.

After years of facilitating workshops and presentations on mentorship, team dynamics, and leadership development, she launched *Rae of Knowledge* (RoK). Her company assists small businesses/organizations and leaders in achieving their goals in a relational way. Through her work, she enjoys helping others achieve build strong work teams, create healthy conflict, and develop their personal leadership styles in a practical, timely manner. Dr. Richardson resides in North Carolina with her spouse and children.

Contact

Email: raeofknowledge@gmail.com
Instagram: @raeofknowledge
Twitter: @sdrichardson09
Website: www.raeofknowledge.com

www.ingramcontent.com/pod-product-compliance
Lightning Source LLC
Chambersburg PA
CBHW021117020426
42331CB00004B/533